# Rediscover

# Wok Cooking

50 New and Amazing Recipes for Wok Lovers

## BY: SOPHIA FREEMAN

© 2019 Sophia Freeman All Rights Reserved

**COPYRIGHTED**

### Liability

This publication is meant as an informational tool. The individual purchaser accepts all liability if damages occur because of following the directions or guidelines set out in this publication. The Author bears no responsibility for reparations caused by the misuse or misinterpretation of the content.

### Copyright

The content of this publication is solely for entertainment purposes and is meant to be purchased by one individual. Permission is not given to any individual who copies, sells or distributes parts or the whole of this publication unless it is explicitly given by the Author in writing.

# My gift to you!

Thank you, cherished reader, for purchasing my book and taking the time to read it. As a special reward for your decision, I would like to offer a gift of free and discounted books directly to your inbox. All you need to do is fill in the box below with your email address and name to start getting amazing offers in the comfort of your own home. You will never miss an offer because a reminder will be sent to you. Never miss a deal and get great deals without having to leave the house! Subscribe now and start saving!

# Table of Contents

Chapter I – Seafood Recipes ..................................................... 8

1) Shrimp and Lobster Stir Fry ............................................. 9

2) Catfish Nuggets with Sriracha Dip ................................ 11

3) Fried Spiced Cod .......................................................... 12

4) Gingered Catfish Nuggets with Sriracha Dip ................. 13

5) Clam and Calamari Stir Fry ........................................... 14

6) Fried Scallions, Red Peppers, and Rice .......................... 16

7) Fried Flounder Bites ..................................................... 18

8) Honey Teriyaki Salmon Bites ........................................ 19

9) Tangy Shrimp with a Chili Cocktail Sauce ..................... 20

10) Spicy Honey Teriyaki Salmon Bites ............................ 21

11) Ham, Shrimp, and Lobster Stir Fry ............................. 23

12) Fried Onions and Calamari ......................................... 25

Chapter II – Chicken, Pork and Beef Recipes ........................ 26

    13) Pork in Oyster Sauce .................................................. 27

    14) Crispy Apple Glaze Honey Teriyaki Baby Back Ribs ... 28

    15) Chicken and Scallions ................................................ 29

    16) Crispy Honey Teriyaki Baby Back Ribs ...................... 31

    17) Celery Seed Chicken .................................................. 32

    18) Citrus Sweet and Sour Nuggets .................................. 34

    19) Shredded Pork ............................................................ 35

    20) Apple Sesame Chicken Nuggets ................................. 36

    21) Pork Pieces and Peppers ............................................ 38

    22) Hot Crispy Honey Fire Drummies .............................. 39

    23) Fried Beef .................................................................. 41

    24) Crispy Honey Fire Drummies ..................................... 42

    25) Beef for Fajitas or Stir-Fry .......................................... 43

    26) Chicken in Peanut Sauce and Lo Mein ........................ 44

    27) Beefy Bok Choy and Peppers ...................................... 45

## Chapter III – Veggies Recipes ... 47

28) Sautéed Mushrooms ... 48

29) Charred Pepper Pieces ... 49

30) Wok Fried Okra ... 50

31) Peppered Beans ... 51

32) Wok Sautéed Bok Choy ... 52

33) Spiced Corn ... 53

34) Citrus Soy Sautéed Bok Choy ... 54

35) Sauced Carrots ... 55

36) Teriyaki Red Peppers ... 56

37) Spicy Onions ... 57

38) Fried Cucumbers ... 58

39) Kicked Up Celery Sticks ... 59

40) Asparagus Fries ... 60

41) Ginger, garlic, and onions, ... 61

42) Sautéed Sweet Potatoes ... 62

Chapter IV – Sausage Recipes ............................................... 63

    43) Sausage and clams ..................................................... 64

    44) Fiery Sausage Stir fry ................................................. 65

    45) Cabbage and Sausage ................................................ 66

    46) Sausage and Chinese Cabbage ..................................... 68

    47) Spicy Ginger Kielbasa and Peppers ............................. 69

    48) Sausage and Ramen Salad ......................................... 70

    49) Sausage Bites with Sriracha Dip.................................. 71

    50) Sausage and Egg Bowl .............................................. 72

    51) 5 Spice Sausage Bites and Dip .................................... 73

Chapter V – Tips ................................................................ 74

About the Author................................................................ 75

Author's Afterthoughts....................................................... 77

# Chapter I – Seafood Recipes

zzzzzzzzzzzzzzzzzzzzzzzzzzzzzzzzzzzzzzzzzzzzzzzzzz

# 1) Shrimp and Lobster Stir Fry

Great for seafood night!

**Serving Size:** 2 servings

**Ingredient List:**

- 2 teaspoons oil
- ½ diced onion
- 2 egg whites
- 2 Diced chili peppers
- ½ cup diced mushroom
- ½ cup EACH: diced shrimp and lobster diced
- ½ teaspoons celery salt and red pepper flakes
- 2-3 cups cooked rice
- 1/3 cup clam juice
- 1 tablespoon orange juice
- 1 teaspoon EACH: orange peel and black pepper

zzzzzzzzzzzzzzzzzzzzzzzzzzzzzzzzzzzzzzzzzzzzzzzz

**Instructions:**

Pour oil in hot wok, sauté aromatics, egg whites, chilies, and mushroom, sauté for 2-3 minutes, add proteins and cook 30-40 secs., add spices, rice, juices, peel and pepper; mix together

# 2) Catfish Nuggets with Sriracha Dip

Great before dinner appetizer's;

**Serving Size:** 20-25

**Ingredient List:**

- 1 teaspoon veg. or canola oil
- ½ teaspoons sesame seed oil
- ½ to 1-pound catfish nuggets
- Season to taste
- ¼ cup cocktail sauce
- ½ Tablespoons sriracha sauce (add more if want it hotter) or chili sauce

zzzzzzzzzzzzzzzzzzzzzzzzzzzzzzzzzzzzzzzzzzzzzzzzz

**Instructions:**

Pour oils in hot wok, cook catfish nuggets 1 approx. 1 min.; in bowl mix together sauces

# 3) Fried Spiced Cod

Great way to make fish sticks!

**Serving Size:** 1 filet

**Ingredient List:**

- 1 tablespoon veg. or canola oil
- ½ Tablespoons EACH: minced onion and minced garlic
- 1 diced scallion
- 1 filet of cod
- 1/3 teaspoons 5 spice seasoning
- 1 egg, beaten
- 1/3 cup panko

zzzzzzzzzzzzzzzzzzzzzzzzzzzzzzzzzzzzzzzzzzzzzzzz

**Instructions:**

Dip filet into beaten egg then spiced panko; pour oil into hot wok followed by aromatics and then filet of fish

# 4) Gingered Catfish Nuggets with Sriracha Dip

For those who like it hot!

**Serving Size:** 20-25

**Ingredient List:**

- 1 teaspoon veg. or canola oil
- ½ teaspoons sesame seed oil
- ½ to 1-pound catfish nuggets
- 1 teaspoon EACH: ground ginger and ground turmeric
- ¼ cup cocktail sauce
- ½ Tablespoons chili sauce (add more if want it hotter)

zzzzzzzzzzzzzzzzzzzzzzzzzzzzzzzzzzzzzzzzzzzzzzzzz

**Instructions:**

Pour oils in hot wok, cook catfish nuggets 1 approx. 1 min.; in bowl mix together sauces

# 5) Clam and Calamari Stir Fry

Great for when you want something "different"!

**Serving Size:** 2 servings

**Ingredient List:**

- 2 teaspoons oil
- 1 piece diced ginger
- 2-3 diced stalks of celery OR ½ teaspoons celery salt/seeds
- 2-3 chopped stalks bok choy
- 1/3 cup worth of sliced mushroom (fav kind & cleaned)
- 1 cup worth fajita style peppers
- ½ cup worth EACH: calamari and clams
- 2-3 cups rice
- ½ cop clam juice
- Pepper to taste

zzzzzzzzzzzzzzzzzzzzzzzzzzzzzzzzzzzzzzzzzzzzzzzz

**Instructions:**

Pour oil in hot wok, add aromatics, mushrooms, and peppers and sauté for 1-2 minutes; add proteins and cook 45 secs to 1 min.; add rice, mix together and stir in calm juice

# 6) Fried Scallions, Red Peppers, and Rice

Large, bay scallions are best but any will work!

**Serving Size:** 2 servings

**Ingredient List:**

- 2 teaspoons veg. or canola oil
- 1 cup all-purpose flour,
- ½ teaspoons smoked paprika
- ½ Tablespoons EACH: minced onions, garlic, and ginger
- Teriyaki red peppers (see recipe in veggie section)
- ½ lbs. scallions
- 2-3 cups cooked rice (jasmine works best)

zzzzzzzzzzzzzzzzzzzzzzzzzzzzzzzzzzzzzzzzzzzzzzzzzz

**Instructions:**

Mix flour and paprika, dip thawed scallions into mix, cover completely, put aside for now

Pour oil in hot wok, sauté aromatics 30-40 seconds and add teriyaki red peppers sautéing for 30-40 seconds; cook prepared scallions 1- 1 ½ minute and remove, mix into cooked veggies and rice

# 7) Fried Flounder Bites

Good in stir fries or fish tacos!

**Serving Size:** 12-15 Bites

**Ingredient List:**

- 2 teaspoons oil
- 2 filets of flounder cut into pieces
- ½ cup flour
- 1 tablespoon panko
- 1/6 teaspoons 5 spice powder

zzzzzzzzzzzzzzzzzzzzzzzzzzzzzzzzzzzzzzzzzzzz

**Instructions:**

Mix flour, panko, and spices together and dip flounder pieces into it; Pour oil into hot wok; cook pieces approx. 1 minute

# 8) Honey Teriyaki Salmon Bites

Great appetizers!

**Serving Size:** 24

**Ingredient List:**

- 2 teaspoons veg. oil or canola oil
- 2-3 salmon filets cut into bite sized pieces (remove any skin)
- 1 tablespoon EACH: soy sauce or Worchester sauce, honey
- ½ Tablespoons EACH: olive oil and brown sugar
- ½ teaspoons black pepper

zzzzzzzzzzzzzzzzzzzzzzzzzzzzzzzzzzzzzzzzzzzzzzz

**Instructions:**

Marinade salmon pieces in soy sauce/Worchester sauce, honey, olive oil, brown sugar, and black pepper; Pour oil into wok, add marinated salmon bites and cook 1 minute

# 9) Tangy Shrimp with a Chili Cocktail Sauce

Great for snacking on during halftime!

**Serving Size:** 20 shrimp

**Ingredient List:**

- 2 teaspoons oil
- 20 large shrimp, cleaned and de-veined'
- 1/3 teaspoons black pepper
- 1/3 cup cocktail sauce
- 1 tablespoon chili sauce

zzzzzzzzzzzzzzzzzzzzzzzzzzzzzzzzzzzzzzzzzzzzzzzzz

**Instructions:**

Pour oil into hot wok, cook shrimp in batches until tender and pink approx. 1-2 minutes; mix together cocktail and chili sauce, chill for 20 minutes before serving

# 10) Spicy Honey Teriyaki Salmon Bites

Great appetizers for heat lovers!

**Serving Size:** 24

**Ingredient List:**

- 2 teaspoons veg. oil or canola oil
- 2-3 salmon filets cut into bite sized pieces (remove any skin)
- 1 tablespoon EACH: soy sauce or Worchester sauce, honey
- ½ Tablespoons EACH: olive oil, brown sugar, sriracha sauce
- ½ teaspoons black pepper

zzzzzzzzzzzzzzzzzzzzzzzzzzzzzzzzzzzzzzzzzzzzzzzz

**Instructions:**

Marinade salmon pieces in soy sauce/Worchester sauce, honey, olive oil, brown sugar, sriracha sauce, and black pepper; Pour oil into wok, add marinated salmon bites and cook 1 minute

# 11) Ham, Shrimp, and Lobster Stir Fry

Great for company!

**Serving Size:** 2 servings

**Ingredient List:**

- 2 teaspoons oil
- 2 egg whites
- ½ diced onion
- ½ diced ginger piece
- 2-3 diced celery sticks OR ½ teaspoons celery salt/seed
- ½ cup diced ham, diced shrimp, and diced lobster
- 2/3 Tablespoons white wine
- 2-3 cups cooked rice

zzzzzzzzzzzzzzzzzzzzzzzzzzzzzzzzzzzzzzzzzzzzzzz

**Instructions:**

Pour oil into hot wok, add egg and aromatics let cook 1-2 minutes and remove; cook proteins until shrimp is pink and tender approx. 45 secs. - 1 minute; add rice and aromatics into proteins and mix

# 12) Fried Onions and Calamari

Fast and delicious!! Make 1 servings

**Ingredient List:**

- 2 teaspoons veg. or canola oil
- ½ cup calamari
- 1/3 cup panko
- 1/3 teaspoons smoked paprika
- ¼ teaspoons black pepper
- ¼ teaspoons EACH: garlic powder, onion powder
- 1 tablespoon all-purpose flour
- Season to taste
- ½ onion, sliced

zzzzzzzzzzzzzzzzzzzzzzzzzzzzzzzzzzzzzzzzzzzzzzzzz

**Instructions:**

Mix flour, panko, paprika, pepper, onion and garlic powders and dip calamari in it; pour oil in hot wok, sauté onions 1 - 1 ½ mins. And add calamari, cook 1-2 minutes

# Chapter II – Chicken, Pork and Beef Recipes

zzzzzzzzzzzzzzzzzzzzzzzzzzzzzzzzzzzzzzzzzzzzzzzzz

# 13) Pork in Oyster Sauce

Great way to use up leftover pork!

**Serving Size:** approx. 2 servings

**Ingredient List:**

- 1-2 teaspoons oil
- ½ cup shredded pork
- ½ teaspoons sesame oil
- ½ teaspoons oyster sauce
- ¼ teaspoons black pepper

zzzzzzzzzzzzzzzzzzzzzzzzzzzzzzzzzzzzzzzzzzzzzzzz

**Instructions:**

Marinate pork in oil, sauce and pepper, cook 3-5 minutes per side depending on size

# 14) Crispy Apple Glaze Honey Teriyaki Baby Back Ribs

Great for those cool weekends spent binge watching!

**Serving Size:** 10

**Ingredient List:**

- 2 teaspoons oil
- 10 baby back ribs
- 1/3 cup soy sauce
- 1 tablespoon Each: apple juice and honey
- 2/3 Tablespoons brown sugar
- ½ Tablespoons apple cider vinegar
- ¼ teaspoons ground cloves, nutmeg, or cinnamon
- ½ teaspoons sesame seed oil and apple pie spice

zzzzzzzzzzzzzzzzzzzzzzzzzzzzzzzzzzzzzzzzzzzzzzz

**Instructions:**

Marinate overnight ribs in ingredients 3-8 then cook 5-6 minutes per side

# 15) Chicken and Scallions

A favorite!

**Serving Size:** 2 servings

**Ingredient List:**

- 1 lbs. chicken cut into strips or cubed
- 1 tablespoon low sodium soy sauce
- ½ Tablespoons honey
- ½ Tablespoons pineapple juice
- 1 teaspoon sesame seed oil
- 2/3 Tablespoons canola oil
- ½ Tablespoons EACH: minced garlic and ginger
- 1/3 teaspoons red pepper flakes
- ¼ teaspoons black pepper
- 4 scallions cut evenly
- ¼ cup cashews or pine nuts

zzzzzzzzzzzzzzzzzzzzzzzzzzzzzzzzzzzzzzzzzzzzzzzz

**Instructions:**

Let first five ingredients marinate overnight; add oil to Wok, add garlic and onion cooking look cook 1 minute, add spices and scallions cooking 1; empty chicken into wok and cook until fully done approx. 4-6 minutes (due to heat discrepancies the cooking time for the chicken might be more or less for you. Please be sure it is thoroughly done as consuming undercooked chicken is hazardous to your health)

# 16) Crispy Honey Teriyaki Baby Back Ribs

Cook in batches of 2 or 3!

**Serving Size:** 10

**Ingredient List:**

- 2 teaspoons oil
- 10 baby back ribs
- 1/3 cup soy sauce
- 1 tablespoon Each: orange or pineapple juice and honey
- 2/3 Tablespoons brown sugar
- ¼ teaspoons ground cloves, nutmeg, or cinnamon
- ½ teaspoons sesame seed oil

zzzzzzzzzzzzzzzzzzzzzzzzzzzzzzzzzzzzzzzzzzzzzzzzz

**Instructions:**

Marinate overnight ribs in ingredients 3-7 then cook 5-6 minutes per side

# 17) Celery Seed Chicken

Like most wok recipes, this one works well with a variety of proteins and veggies!

**Serving Size:** 2-3 servings

**Ingredient List:**

- 1 lbs. chicken cubes
- ½ teaspoons white wine
- 1 teaspoon sesame seed oil
- ½ teaspoons celery seed
- 1/3 teaspoons black pepper
- ½ Tablespoons peanut oil
- 4 diced scallions
- 1/3 cup diced shiitake mushrooms
- 1 recipe fried broccoli (see veggies section for recipe)
- 2-3 cups white or jasmine rice

zzzzzzzzzzzzzzzzzzzzzzzzzzzzzzzzzzzzzzzzzzzzzzzz

**Instructions:**

Marinate first 5 ingredients overnight in refrigerator; empty all marinades contents in hot wok, cook 4-5 minutes and remove; add peanut oil, sauté mushrooms and scallions 1-2 minutes and remove, place all on top of rice and serve.

# 18) Citrus Sweet and Sour Nuggets

A great lunch treats for children!

**Serving Size:** 8

**Ingredient List:**

- 2 teaspoons oil
- Boneless skinless chicken breast or thigh cut into 8 pieces
- 1 teaspoon soy sauce
- ½ EACH: Tablespoons pineapple juice AND honey AND brown sugar

zzzzzzzzzzzzzzzzzzzzzzzzzzzzzzzzzzzzzzzzzzzzzzzzz

**Instructions:**

Add ingredients 2 - 4 into bag and marinate 4-8 hours; pour oil into hot wok, cook marinated chicken 4-6 minutes per side

# 19) Shredded Pork

Great in stir fries, soups, and stews!

**Serving Size:** 2 cups worth

**Ingredient List:**

- 2/3 veg. or canola oil
- ½ Tablespoons Each onion sliced and piece of ginger sliced
- ¼ cup mushrooms, diced
- 1 lbs. pork
- 1 tablespoon soy sauce or Worchester sauce
- ¼ cup pineapple juice
- ¼ teaspoons black pepper

zzzzzzzzzzzzzzzzzzzzzzzzzzzzzzzzzzzzzzzzzzzzzzz

**Instructions:**

Marinate pork overnight in ingredient 5-7; pour oil into hot wok, add aromatics and mushrooms and sauté approx. 1- 1 ½ minutes; cook pork 5 minutes (2 ½ on each side), remove from heat and shred, return, add more oil if necessary, and cook 3-5 more minutes continuously moving around.

# 20) Apple Sesame Chicken Nuggets

Great for a quick protein pick-me-up!

**Serving Size:** 8 nuggets

**Ingredient List:**

- 2 teaspoons Oil
- ½ Tablespoons butter and brown sugar
- Chicken boneless, skinless breasts or thighs cut into 8 pieces
- ½ Tablespoons sesame seed oil
- 1 tablespoon apple cider vinegar
- 1/3 teaspoons EACH: onion powder and red pepper flakes

zzzzzzzzzzzzzzzzzzzzzzzzzzzzzzzzzzzzzzzzzzzzzzzzz

**Instructions:**

Place cut chicken into a bag along with sesame oil, vinegar, and onion powder; let marinade 4 hours

Pour oil into hot wok, let butter melt, add brown sugar, cook marinade chicken 4-6 minutes per side

# 21) Pork Pieces and Peppers

A smooth apple flavor!

**Serving Size:** 2 servings

**Ingredient List:**

- 2 teaspoons veg. or canola oil
- ½ Tablespoons Each onion sliced, 2 cloves of garlic diced, and piece of ginger sliced
- ¼ cup mushrooms, diced
- 1 lbs. pork
- 1 teaspoon sesame seed oil
- ½ Tablespoons: brown sugar
- 1 tablespoon soy sauce or Worchester sauce
- ¼ cup apple juice
- ¼ teaspoons black pepper

zzzzzzzzzzzzzzzzzzzzzzzzzzzzzzzzzzzzzzzzzzzzzzz

**Instructions:**

Marinate pork overnight in ingredients 5-9; pour oil into hot wok, add aromatics and sauté approx. 1- 1 ½ min. and remove; and cook pork 3-4 minutes on each side.

# 22) Hot Crispy Honey Fire Drummies

Makes small gatherings even more memorable!

**Serving Size:** 10-12

**Ingredient List:**

- 2-3 teaspoons oil
- 10-12 drummies
- ½ teaspoons EACH: onion powder, garlic salt, white pepper
- 1/3 teaspoons 5 spice powder
- 1 teaspoon sesame seed oil
- 1 teaspoon soy sauce
- 1 teaspoon brown sugar
- ½ Tablespoons honey
- ½ Tablespoons pineapple juice

zzzzzzzzzzzzzzzzzzzzzzzzzzzzzzzzzzzzzzzzzzzzzzzzz

**Instructions:**

Marinade drummies overnight in ingredients 3-9; cook 4-5 minutes turning occasionally

# 23) Fried Beef

Add the perfect bit of flavor to a beef soup or stew!

**Serving Size:** approx. 2 cups

**Ingredient List:**

- 2 teaspoons veg. oil or canola oil
- 1 lb. beef for stew
- ½ cup all-purpose flour
- 1 teaspoon EACH: paprika, black pepper, onion powder, and garlic powder
- 1 teaspoon olive oil AND sesame oil
- ¼ Tablespoons red pepper flakes
- 1 tablespoon Worchester sauce
- 1 tablespoon apple cider vinegar

zzzzzzzzzzzzzzzzzzzzzzzzzzzzzzzzzzzzzzzzzzzzzzzzz

**Instructions:**

Marinate beef overnight in ingredients 3-7, roll in flour, and cook 3-5 minutes on each side

# 24) Crispy Honey Fire Drummies

Makes small gatherings even more memorable!

**Serving Size:** 10-12

**Ingredient List:**

- 2-3 teaspoons oil
- 10-12 drummies
- ½ teaspoons EACH: onion powder, garlic salt, red pepper flakes or white pepper
- 1 teaspoon sesame seed oil
- 1 teaspoon soy sauce
- 1 teaspoon brown sugar
- ½ Tablespoons honey
- ½ Tablespoons pineapple juice

zzzzzzzzzzzzzzzzzzzzzzzzzzzzzzzzzzzzzzzzzzzzzzzz

**Instructions:**

Marinade drummies overnight in ingredients 3-8; cook 4-5 minutes turning occasionally

# 25) Beef for Fajitas or Stir-Fry

Add the perfect bit of flavor to a beef soup or stew!

**Serving Size:** approx. 2 cups

**Ingredient List:**

- 2 teaspoons veg. oil or canola oil
- 1 lb. beef strips
- ½ teaspoons EACH: onion powder and garlic powder and ginger powder
- 1 teaspoon EACH: black pepper
- ½ Tablespoons sesame oil
- ¼ Tablespoons red pepper flakes or jalapeno powder
- 1 teaspoon Worchester sauce

zzzzzzzzzzzzzzzzzzzzzzzzzzzzzzzzzzzzzzzzzzzzzzzzzz

**Instructions:**

Marinate beef overnight in ingredients 3-7, roll in flour, and cook 2- 3 minutes on each side

# 26) Chicken in Peanut Sauce and Lo Mein

Easy weeknight dinner!

**Serving Size:** 2 servings

**Ingredient List:**

- 2 teaspoons oil
- 1 cup shredded chicken
- ½ - 1 tablespoon peanut sauce
- 1 can lo mien vegetables
- 1 package lo mien noodles

zzzzzzzzzzzzzzzzzzzzzzzzzzzzzzzzzzzzzzzzzzzzzzzzz

**Instructions:**

Mix peanut sauce and chicken together, cook in oil 30 seconds - 1 minute, add veggies and cook 2-4 more minutes; cook noodles according to package directions, drain, and mix into chicken and veggies

# 27) Beefy Bok Choy and Peppers

Makes a hearty meal!

**Serving Size:** 2 servings

**Ingredient List:**

- 2 teaspoons oil
- ½ onion diced
- 1-piece ginger diced
- 2 cloves garlic sliced thin
- ½ teaspoons red pepper flakes, and black pepper
- 1 lb. beef strips
- 1 tablespoon Hoisin sauce (optional)
- 2 cups bok choy
- 1 cup worth of fajita style peppers
- 2-3 cups jasmine rice

zzzzzzzzzzzzzzzzzzzzzzzzzzzzzzzzzzzzzzzzzzzzzzzzz

**Instructions:**

Pour oil into hot wok, sauté aromatics 1 minute along with peppers and bok choy, remove; cook beef with red pepper flakes and pepper 2-3 minutes, remove and add into pepper's & rice mix

# Chapter III – Veggies Recipes

zzzzzzzzzzzzzzzzzzzzzzzzzzzzzzzzzzzzzzzzzzzzzzzzzz

# 28) Sautéed Mushrooms

Here we use shitake mushrooms but use any kind you wish!

**Serving Size:** 2 servings

**Ingredient List:**

- 2 teaspoons oil
- 4 shitake mushrooms, chopped
- ½ Tablespoons soy sauce
- ½ teaspoons onion powder and garlic powder and black pepper

zzzzzzzzzzzzzzzzzzzzzzzzzzzzzzzzzzzzzzzzzzzzzzz

**Instructions:**

Marinate mushroom pieces in soy sauce, onion powder, pepper, and garlic powder; cook in oil 2-3 minutes

## 29) Charred Pepper Pieces

Great addition to stir-fries!

**Serving Size:** 6-8 pieces

**Ingredient List:**

- 1 teaspoon oil
- 2 bell peppers cut into 6-8 long and wide pieces

zzzzzzzzzzzzzzzzzzzzzzzzzzzzzzzzzzzzzzzzzzzzzzzz

**Instructions:**

Pour oil into hot wok and put in pepper pieces cook until tender and starting to char 4-7 minutes (due to heat discrepancies times may differ)

# 30) Wok Fried Okra

Quick, inexpensive, and great for snaking or in won tons!

**Serving Size:** 2-3 servings

**Ingredient List:**

- ¼ cup peanut oil
- 1 bag frozen okra
- 1 egg, beaten
- 1 cup panko

zzzzzzzzzzzzzzzzzzzzzzzzzzzzzzzzzzzzzzzzzzzzzz

**Instructions:**

Dip thawed pieces of okra into egg (if pieces are hard to dip try inserting a toothpick into the middle), roll or swirl into panko, fry in peanut oil till golden brown 2-4 minutes

# 31) Peppered Beans

Goes great with all types of proteins!

**Serving Size:** ½ cup worth

**Ingredient List:**

- 1 teaspoon oil
- ½ teaspoons sesame seed oil
- ½ cup green beans, drained
- 1/3 teaspoons EACH: red pepper flakes, white pepper, and 5 spice powder
- 1 teaspoon teriyaki sauce

zzzzzzzzzzzzzzzzzzzzzzzzzzzzzzzzzzzzzzzzzzzzzzz

**Instructions:**

Pour oils into hot wok, add beans and sauté for 30 secs, and remaining ingredients and cook another minute

# 32) Wok Sautéed Bok Choy

Good on its own or in soups!

**Serving Size:** 2-3 servings

**Ingredient List:**

- 2 Tablespoons veg. oil
- 2 cups worth of chopped bok choy (3x3 is a good size)
- 1 tablespoon soy sauce

zzzzzzzzzzzzzzzzzzzzzzzzzzzzzzzzzzzzzzzzzzzzzzzzzz

**Instructions:**

Heat oil and insert bok choy pieces (work in batches as to not crowd it) and add soy sauce; add another ½ Tablespoons of soy sauce for next batch

## 33) Spiced Corn

Also a great addition to casseroles!

**Serving Size:** ½ cup worth

**Ingredient List:**

- 1 teaspoon oil
- ½ teaspoons sesame seed oil
- ½ cup whole kernel corn, drained
- 1/3 teaspoons EACH: red pepper flakes and black pepper
- 1 teaspoon teriyaki sauce

zzzzzzzzzzzzzzzzzzzzzzzzzzzzzzzzzzzzzzzzzzzzzzz

**Instructions:**

Pour oils into hot wok, add corn sauté for 30 secs, add remaining ingredients and cook another minute

# 34) Citrus Soy Sautéed Bok Choy

Great side dish!

**Serving Size:** 2-3 servings

**Ingredient List:**

- 2 Tablespoons veg. oil
- 2 cups worth of chopped bok choy (3x3 is a good size)
- 1 tablespoon citrus soy sauce

zzzzzzzzzzzzzzzzzzzzzzzzzzzzzzzzzzzzzzzzzzzzzzzz

**Instructions:**

Heat oil and insert bok choy pieces (work in batches as to not crowd it) and add soy sauce; add another ½ Tablespoons of soy sauce for next batch

# 35) Sauced Carrots

Great as a side dish or in salads, soups, or stews!

**Serving Size:** 20

**Ingredient List:**

- 1 teaspoon oil
- ½ Tablespoons butter
- ½ onion sliced
- 1 tablespoon EACH: minced garlic and ginger
- 20 carrot pieces or baby carrots
- ½ EACH: Tablespoons soy sauce and honey
- ½ teaspoons vanilla extract

zzzzzzzzzzzzzzzzzzzzzzzzzzzzzzzzzzzzzzzzzzzzzzzz

**Instructions:**

Pour oil and butter into hot wok, cook onion 1-2 minutes and add garlic and ginger and cook 1 more minute, remove; add carrots, soy sauce, honey and vanilla extract and cook 1-2 minutes, remove and mix together

# 36) Teriyaki Red Peppers

Great for snaking!

**Serving Size:** 2-3 servings

**Ingredient List:**

- ¼ cup veg. oil
- 1 cup worth roasted red pepper pieces
- 1 tablespoon low sodium soy sauce
- ½ Tablespoons honey
- 1/3 Tablespoons pineapple juice
- 1/3 teaspoons sesame seed oil
- Onion strips (optional)

zzzzzzzzzzzzzzzzzzzzzzzzzzzzzzzzzzzzzzzzzzzzzz

**Instructions:**

Let peppers marinate overnight in plastic bag in fridge in ingredients 2-6; warm oil over medium high heat and sauté red pepper 2-3 minutes

# 37) Spicy Onions

Great on their own or in soups and stews!

**Serving Size:** approx. 1 cup worth or 2-3 servings

**Ingredient List:**

- 2 teaspoons oil
- 1 onion sliced
- 1 teaspoon EACH: butter and brown sugar
- 1/3 teaspoons EACH: black pepper, red pepper flakes and garlic salt,
- 1 teaspoon soy sauce

zzzzzzzzzzzzzzzzzzzzzzzzzzzzzzzzzzzzzzzzzzzzzzz

**Instructions:**

Pour oil into hot wok, put in onion, butter and brown sugar, sauté 1-2 minutes; add peppers and spices and soy sauce

# 38) Fried Cucumbers

Fast and easy snacks!

**Serving Size:** 20

**Ingredient List:**

- 2 teaspoons veg. oil or canola oil
- 2 sliced cucumbers
- 1/3 cup panko
- 1 tablespoon all-purpose flour
- 1/3 teaspoons black pepper

zzzzzzzzzzzzzzzzzzzzzzzzzzzzzzzzzzzzzzzzzzzzzzzz

**Instructions:**

Mix flour, panko, pepper, and dip cucumbers into it, and fry in hot oil for 1 minute or until golden brown

# 39) Kicked Up Celery Sticks

Great for dipping!

**Serving Size:** 20 sticks

**Ingredient List:**

- 2 teaspoons oil
- 20 celery sticks
- 1/3 teaspoons red pepper flakes, white pepper, and 5 spice powder

zzzzzzzzzzzzzzzzzzzzzzzzzzzzzzzzzzzzzzzzzzzzzzz

**Instructions:**

Pour oil into hot wok, in small bowl mix together peppers and spices, sprinkle over celery, put into wok and sauté 1-2 minutes

# 40) Asparagus Fries

A great way to eat your vegetables!

**Serving Size:** 10 fries

**Ingredient List:**

- 1 teaspoon oil
- 10 asparagus pieces
- ½ cup panko
- ½ teaspoons red pepper flakes

zzzzzzzzzzzzzzzzzzzzzzzzzzzzzzzzzzzzzzzzzzzzzzzz

**Instructions:**

Mix together panko and red pepper flakes, roll asparagus in it and place in hot oil, and cook 1-2 minutes per side

# 41) Ginger, garlic, and onions,

A good base for a vegetarian soup or stir fry!

**Serving Size:** approx. 2-3 cups worth

**Ingredient List:**

- 2 teaspoons oil
- 2 pieces thinly sliced ginger
- 1 onion sliced
- 3 cloves of garlic thinly sliced
- 2/3 Tablespoons soy sauce
- 1/3 teaspoons red pepper flakes AND black pepper

zzzzzzzzzzzzzzzzzzzzzzzzzzzzzzzzzzzzzzzzzzzzzzz

**Instructions:**

Marinate ingredients 2-6 overnight and cook 2-3 minutes

# 42) Sautéed Sweet Potatoes

Goes great with crisp ribs!

**Serving Size:** 2 servings

**Ingredient List:**

- 2 teaspoons oil
- ½ onion sliced
- 1 piece or ginger cut into pieces
- 1 cup worth fajita style peppers
- 2 sweet potatoes cut into bite sized pieces
- 1/3 teaspoons black pepper
- 1 teaspoon soy sauce (optional)

zzzzzzzzzzzzzzzzzzzzzzzzzzzzzzzzzzzzzzzzzzzzzzzzz

**Instructions:**

Over oil in hot wok sauté onion and ginger 2-3 minutes, remove, cook peppers 2-3 minutes and push aside, add sweet potato pieces and add pepper and soy sauce, sauté 2-3 minutes, add onions and ginger and mix

# Chapter IV – Sausage Recipes

zzzzzzzzzzzzzzzzzzzzzzzzzzzzzzzzzzzzzzzzzzzzzzzzzzz

# 43) Sausage and clams

Great for those too hot for cooking nights!

**Serving Size:** 2 servings

**Ingredient List:**

- 2 teaspoons oil
- 2 egg white
- 1 diced onion
- 1 diced piece of ginger
- 2-3 sliced celery stalks OR ½ teaspoons celery salt/seeds
- 1 package kielbasa, sliced
- 1/3 - ½ cup clams, with juice
- 2-3 cups jasmine rice
- Soy sauce (optional)

zzzzzzzzzzzzzzzzzzzzzzzzzzzzzzzzzzzzzzzzzzzzzzzzzzz

**Instructions:**

Pour oil into hot wok, cook egg white and aromatics 1 min. and remove; cook proteins 1 minute and add rice and aromatics, mix together

# 44) Fiery Sausage Stir fry

Great for impromptu company!

**Serving Size:** 2-3 servings

**Ingredient List:**

- 2 teaspoons oil
- ½ onion sliced
- 2-3 stalks bok choy chopped
- ½ teaspoons lemon peel or orange peel, 5 spice powder, celery salt/seed
- 1 tablespoon minced garlic and ginger
- ½ package kielbasa sliced
- 2-3 cups cooked rice

zzzzzzzzzzzzzzzzzzzzzzzzzzzzzzzzzzzzzzzzzzzzzzzzzz

**Instructions:**

Pour oil into hot wok, cook till onion begins to caramelize, add bok choy, spices, garlic and ginger; push around 30-40 secs, add kielbasa and rice

# 45) Cabbage and Sausage

Great hot or cold!

**Serving Size:** 2 servings

**Ingredient List:**

- 2 teaspoons veg. or canola oil
- ½ onion diced
- ¼ cup diced celery
- 1/3 teaspoons red pepper flakes
- ¼ teaspoons soy sauce
- 1 ½ cup sliced cabbage
- 1 ½ cup bok choy
- ½ package sliced kielbasa
- 2-3 cups cooked egg noodles

zzzzzzzzzzzzzzzzzzzzzzzzzzzzzzzzzzzzzzzzzzzzzzzzz

**Instructions:**

Pour oil in hot wok, add onion, celery, red pepper flakes, soy sauce, and sauté one minute; push aside and add cabbage and kale, if needed add another 1 teaspoon of oil, cook 45 seconds and push aside; add sausage cook 2-3 minutes and mix in cooked egg noodles mixing all ingredients together

# 46) Sausage and Chinese Cabbage

Great for outdoor potlucks!

**Serving Size:** 5-7 servings

**Ingredient List:**

- 2 teaspoons of oil
- ½ onion sliced
- 1 diced piece of ginger
- I head of Chinese cabbage
- 1 package spicy kielbasa sliced and 1 pack regular kielbasa sliced
- 1/3 teaspoons red pepper flakes and black pepper
- ½ Tablespoons soy sauce

zzzzzzzzzzzzzzzzzzzzzzzzzzzzzzzzzzzzzzzzzzzzzzzzzz

**Instructions:**

Pour hot oil into wok, caramelize onion by letting cook approx. 2-3 minutes, add ginger, proteins peppers, and soy sauce, let cook 3-4 minutes

# 47) Spicy Ginger Kielbasa and Peppers

Also great with various seafood's!

**Serving Size:** 2 servings

**Ingredient List:**

- 2teaspoons veg. or canola oil
- ½ teaspoons minced ginger
- ½ Tablespoons minced garlic
- 1 cup fajita style peppers
- ½ package sliced spicy kielbasa
- 2-3 cups rice (jasmine is best)

zzzzzzzzzzzzzzzzzzzzzzzzzzzzzzzzzzzzzzzzzzzzzzz

**Instructions:**

Pour oil in hot wok, add ginger and garlic and sauté 30 seconds, and peppers, cook 30-45 seconds and remove to plate; if necessary, cook sausage 2-3 minutes, and mix together

# 48) Sausage and Ramen Salad

A great side for a bbq!

**Serving Size:** approx. 2-3 cups worth or 2-3 servings

**Ingredient List:**

- 2 teaspoons oil
- ½ package kielbasa sliced or ½ package cocktail franks
- ½ package pepperoni bits
- ½ lb. diced medium shrimp
- ½ cup diced lobster
- ½ teaspoons EACH: red pepper flakes and lemon peel
- ½ Tablespoons EACH: clam juice and white wine
- 1 cup worth of authentic Japanese ramen noodles

zzzzzzzzzzzzzzzzzzzzzzzzzzzzzzzzzzzzzzzzzzzzzzzz

**Instructions:**

Pour oil into hot wok, working in batches cook proteins 1-3 minutes, add spices, juices, and mix in ramen

# 49) Sausage Bites with Sriracha Dip

Can use either sliced kielbasa pieces or cocktail franks!

**Serving Size:** 24

**Ingredient List:**

- 2 teaspoons veg. or canola oil
- 24 sausage bites (cook in batches)
- 1/3 cup ketchup
- 1 teaspoon Worchester sauce
- ½ Tablespoons sriracha sauce or chili sauce

zzzzzzzzzzzzzzzzzzzzzzzzzzzzzzzzzzzzzzzzzzzzzzzzz

**Instructions:**

Pour oil inn hot wok and cook sausage bites 1 minute; mix ketchup, Worchester sauce, and sriracha or chili sauce and serve

# 50) Sausage and Egg Bowl

Great any time of day!

**Serving Size:** 2 servings

**Ingredient List:**

- 1 teaspoon oil
- ½ diced onion
- ¼ cup diced bell pepper
- 2 eggs
- 1 roll frozen breakfast sausage crumbled
- ¼ teaspoons black pepper
- 1/6 teaspoons smoked paprika or turmeric
- 2-3 cup jasmine rice or 10-inch burrito shells

zzzzzzzzzzzzzzzzzzzzzzzzzzzzzzzzzzzzzzzzzzzzzzzzz

**Instructions:**

Add oil to hot wok, cook onion, peppers, eggs (be sure to keep "breaking up" eggs as they don't clump together) cook 1 minute and add sausage and spices, sauté 2 minutes

# 51) 5 Spice Sausage Bites and Dip

For the heat lovers in your crowd!

**Serving Size:** 20-24

**Ingredient List:**

- 2 teaspoons veg. or canola oil
- 1/3 -½ teaspoons 5 spice powder
- 24 sausage bites (cook in batches)
- 1/3 cup ketchup
- 1 teaspoon Worchester sauce
- ½ Tablespoons sriracha sauce or chili sauce

zzzzzzzzzzzzzzzzzzzzzzzzzzzzzzzzzzzzzzzzzzzzzzzz

**Instructions:**

Pour oil in hot wok, add 5 spice, and cook sausage bites 1 minute; mix ketchup, Worchester sauce, and sriracha or chili sauce and serve

# Chapter V – Tips

1. Use oils with high cooking temps such as canola or peanut

2. Preheat before adding oil

3. Pour oil slowly down the side and swirl

4. Cook aromatics, such as garlic and onions, first and let their oils seep into the cooking oil to add flavor to remaining ingredients

5. Let meat sear untouched for 45 secs – 1 min after putting in wok

6. Try to cut veggies to same or similar size to ensure and encourage even cooking

7. Continuously flip food to encourage even cooking

8. Dry proteins and veggies before introducing into Wok

9. Scrub before using to remove residues

10. Some woks need seasoning to avoid this buy a non-stick carbon Wok; it works just as good!

# About the Author

A native of Albuquerque, New Mexico, Sophia Freeman found her calling in the culinary arts when she enrolled at the Sante Fe School of Cooking. Freeman decided to take a year after graduation and travel around Europe, sampling the cuisine from small bistros and family owned restaurants from Italy to Portugal. Her bubbly personality and inquisitive nature made her popular with the locals in the villages and when she finished her trip and came home, she had made friends for life in the places she had visited. She also came home with a deeper understanding of European cuisine.

Freeman went to work at one of Albuquerque's 5-star restaurants as a sous-chef and soon worked her way up to head chef. The restaurant began to feature Freeman's original dishes as specials on the menu and soon after, she began to write e-books with her recipes. Sophia's dishes mix local flavours with European inspiration making them irresistible to the diners in her restaurant and the online community.

Freeman's experience in Europe didn't just teach her new ways of cooking, but also unique methods of presentation. Using rich sauces, crisp vegetables and meat cooked to perfection, she creates a stunning display as well as a delectable dish. She has won many local awards for her cuisine and she continues to delight her diners with her culinary masterpieces.

* * * ★ ★ ★ ★ ★ ★ ★ * *

# Author's Afterthoughts

I want to convey my big thanks to all of my readers who have taken the time to read my book. Readers like you make my work so rewarding and I cherish each and every one of you.

Grateful cannot describe how I feel when I know that someone has chosen my work over all of the choices available online. I hope you enjoyed the book as much as I enjoyed writing it.

Feedback from my readers is how I grow and learn as a chef and an author. Please take the time to let me know your thoughts by leaving a review on Amazon so I and your fellow readers can learn from your experience.

*My deepest thanks,*

**Sophia Freeman**

**Subscribe to the Newsletter!**

https://sophia.subscribemenow.com/

* * * * ★ ★ ★ ★ ★ * * *

Printed in Great
Britain
by Amazon